BABYSITTING

Babysitting SKILLS

TRAITS AND TRAINING FOR SUCCESS

by Wendy Ann Mattox
Consultant: Beth Lapp
Certified Babysitting Training Instructor

Capstone press

Mankato, Minnesota

Snap Books are published by Capstone Press,
151 Good Counsel Drive, P.O. Box 669, Mankato, Minnesota 56002.
www.capstonepress.com

Library of Congress Cataloging-in-Publication Data
Mattox, Wendy Ann.
    Babysitting skills: traits and training for success / Wendy Ann Mattox.
    p.cm.—(Snap books. Babysitting)
    Summary: "A guide for pre-teens and teens on the skills needed to
babysit"—Provided by publisher.
    Includes bibliographical references and index.
    ISBN-13: 978-0-7368-6466-4 (hardcover)
    ISBN-10: 0-7368-6466-0 (hardcover)
    1. Babysitting—Juvenile literature. 2. Babysitters—Training
of—Juvenile literature. I. Title. II. Series.
HQ769.5.M383 2007
649'.10248—dc22   2006001736

Editor: Becky Viaene
Designer: Jennifer Bergstrom
Photo Researcher/Photo Editor: Kelly Garvin

Photo Credits:
Capstone Press/ Karon Dubke, 7 (pacifier), 24 (all objects); Capstone Press/TJ Thoraldson Digital Photography,
cover, 6 (first aid kit), 7, 8–9, 20–21, 22–23, 26–27; Corbis/Laura Dwight, 15; Corbis/LWA-Dann Tardif, 19;
Corbis/zefa/S. Hammid, 28; Corbis/zefa/Tom Stewart, 4–5; Image Source/elektraVision, 25; PhotoEdit Inc./
Mary Kate Denny, 11; SuperStock/age fotostock, 12–13; SuperStock/Kwame Zikomo, 16–17; Wendy Ann Mattox, 32

1 2 3 4 5 6 11 10 09 08 07 06

Table of Contents

A Super Sitter

> **Are you responsible, honest, and patient? Have you taken CPR and first aid training? Are you ready to watch multiple children or deal with illness and injuries?**

If you answered "yes" to these questions, you are probably ready to begin babysitting. From diapering a baby to handling misbehavior, babysitters need many skills.

This book will teach you what skills you need, why you need them, and how to improve them. Combine the right skills with training, and you've got what it takes to be a super sitter!

Training and Experience

You didn't learn to read or ride a bike in only one day. And you won't turn into a successful babysitter overnight, either.

You got better at riding a bike by practicing. Becoming a good babysitter takes practice too. Begin your training by taking a babysitting class. The class should teach you diapering skills, feeding skills, safety tips, and first aid procedures. Also take safety classes that teach CPR and the Heimlich maneuver. After taking babysitting and safety classes, you'll have the skills to handle most situations, even emergencies.

The next step of your training involves getting some babysitting experience. Offer to babysit siblings or relatives. Practice and proper training will make your job easier.

First Aid

Helpful Hint

Parents may ask you to cook or make simple snacks while you're babysitting. Practice at home so you're prepared.

Honesty and More

You may already have some of the best traits a babysitter can have. Now you just need to practice using them.

Honesty

Parents will trust you to babysit if you're honest. Never lie to parents about what happened while they were gone. The children will tell their parents that you lied and you won't be asked back to babysit. You also need to be honest with children. Don't disappoint them by making promises you can't keep.

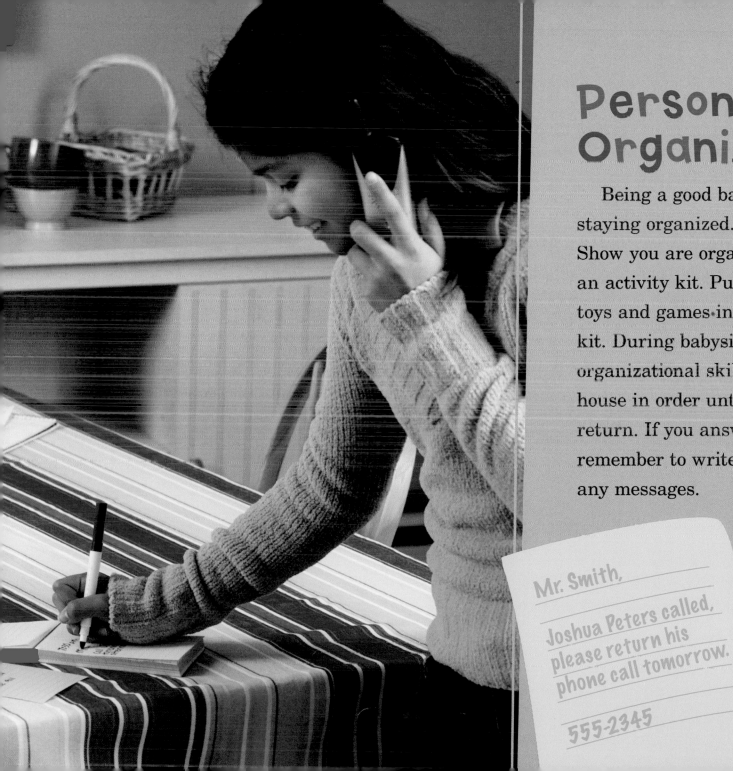

Personal Organization

Being a good babysitter means staying organized. Come prepared. Show you are organized by bringing an activity kit. Put age-appropriate toys and games inside the activity kit. During babysitting jobs, use organizational skills to keep the house in order until the parents return. If you answer the phone, remember to write down any messages.

Mr. Smith,

Joshua Peters called, please return his phone call tomorrow.

555-2345

9

Dependability

Show you're a dependable babysitter by always being on time for jobs. Babysitters who show up late likely won't be asked to babysit again.

Also, a dependable babysitter doesn't cancel a babysitting job to do something else. If you must cancel because you're sick, give as much notice as possible.

Listening Skills

Listening is one of the most important parts of being a good babysitter. Write down parents' instructions if you don't think you'll remember them. If you don't listen closely, you may let a child stay up past his bedtime. Or you may not remember which foods a child is allergic to, which could be life-threatening. Using listening skills helps keep everyone happy and safe.

Helpful Hint

You can become a better listener by:

* Keeping good eye contact
* Repeating what was said
* Avoiding distractions
* Not interrupting
* Asking questions

Patience

Young children will take longer than you to do simple tasks, such as tying their shoes. They learn by doing things by themselves, which may be frustrating for you and them. Stay patient by talking calmly, taking a deep breath, and counting to 10.

You also need patience to handle accidents, like spilled juice, and misbehavior. If you aren't patient, babysitting probably isn't the right job for you.

Diapering and Feeding Babies

Although babies are small, taking care of them can be a big job.

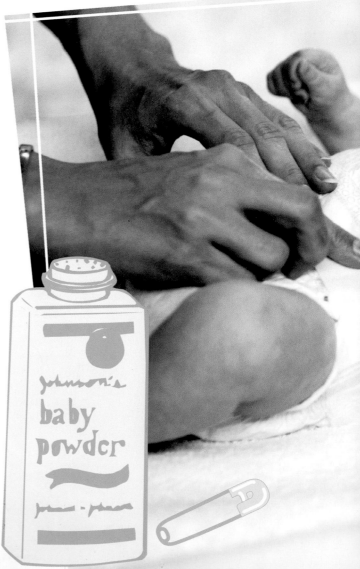

You would love to watch the neighbor's cute baby. To watch a baby, you will need to have plenty of patience, energy, and experience. Without these skills, babysitting an infant will be very frustrating. You will also need diaper-changing and bottle-feeding skills.

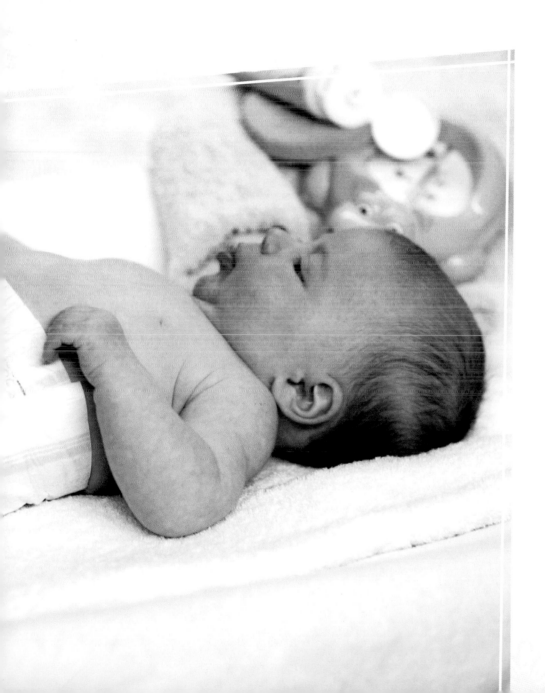

HOW TO CHANGE A DIAPER

Before you begin changing the baby's diaper, grab a diaper and wipes or a wet washcloth. Once the supplies are close by, follow these simple steps:

1. Gently lay the baby on her back on top of a covered changing area. Take off the dirty diaper and move it away from the baby.

2. Clean the baby's bottom with a baby wipe or warm washcloth. Always wipe from front to back.

3. Put a clean diaper on the baby.

4. Check to make sure the diaper isn't too tight or too loose.

5. Put the baby in a safe place, such as a crib. Then throw the diaper away and wash your hands.

13

How to Mix a Bottle and Feed a Baby

If the baby cries, don't panic! Instead, stay calm while determining the reason for the crying. Does she want to be held? Is she hungry? Try feeding her a bottle.

1. Place the baby in a playpen or crib while you wash your hands. Gather a bottle, formula, and water.
2. Mix the formula in the bottle according to directions on the formula can.
3. Heat the bottle by putting it into a container filled with warm water for a few minutes. Don't warm the bottle in the microwave. Microwaves can heat bottles unevenly, causing some of the formula to get too hot.
4. Check the formula temperature by squeezing a few drops on your wrist.
5. Put a bib on the baby to protect her clothing.
6. While feeding, hold the baby in your arms, with her head higher than her stomach. Remember to take breaks from feeding to burp the baby.

BURPING BABIES

One of the most important parts of feeding babies is getting them to burp. Here's how:

1. After every 2 ounces (0.06 liters) a baby drinks, stop feeding and try to burp him.

2. Hold the baby in your lap or with his head over your shoulder. Place a cloth on your lap or shoulder to catch any spit-up.

3. Use your hand to gently pat or rub his back.

4. If the baby doesn't burp after a few minutes, continue feeding him.

Staying Alert

One- to three-year-olds have short attention spans and are full of energy. One of the most important skills when watching toddlers is to be alert!

Never take your eyes off toddlers. If you're not watching, they could pinch their fingers, swallow small toys, or tumble down steps. Watch closely as curious toddlers explore. Encourage them to try things themselves and wait patiently until they ask for help.

Be prepared for tantrums and constant use of the words "mine" and "no." At this age, toddlers will test your patience. Stay calm and take charge. Toddlers feel safe when you enforce the rules.

Thoughtful and Creative

"Why?" is a common question asked many times each day by children ages 4 to 6. Preschoolers are eager to learn more about the world around them.

Preschoolers will constantly keep you thinking. By answering their questions, you can teach them how things work.

To babysit preschoolers you'll need to be creative. Prepare to pretend. Pretending and other imaginative play helps preschoolers develop creativity, practice rules, and understand emotions.

Preschoolers love choices, like picking which pajamas to wear or what game to play.

CRAYONS

Responsible and Encouraging

Babysitting older children can be more challenging than watching younger kids.

By age 7, most children get angry if they think they're being treated like a baby. They want to be treated like a grown-up and enjoy doing things independently. Allow them some privacy to do activities alone. But be responsible and make sure that the activities, like watching TV, are age-appropriate.

WHAT WOULD YOU DO?
The boy you're babysitting refuses to go to bed. He says only babies go to bed early and begs to stay up an hour later.

Even though children at this age may want time alone, they also enjoy spending time with you. Be generous and let children make some decisions, like which games to play.

Children at this age are constantly seeking approval and need your encouragement. Praise them when they do something well. Set a good example by being responsible and following the rules. Kids will look up to you as a role model.

SIMPLE SOLUTION

Help him prepare for bed. One hour before bedtime, read and do other relaxing activities with him. Be responsible and assertive. Don't let the child stay up past his bedtime.

Problem-solving Skills

Babysitting children of different genders and ages can be difficult. Avoid hurt feelings by using problem-solving skills to help make everyone feel happy.

When you're babysitting multiple kids, be fair and give each child equal attention. Never choose one child's side. Use the problem-solving process to end arguments. Start by asking everyone to think about the problem. Then respect everyone as they discuss the problem. Work together to think of solutions. Pick the best solution, which may mean compromising.

WHAT WOULD YOU DO?

One of the boys you're babysitting wants to play Candy Land. His older brother says he doesn't want to play. He wants to play cards instead.

SIMPLE SOLUTION

Suggest a compromise. Encourage the boys to set a timer and play both games for a certain amount of time. Or suggest they pick a different game or activity that they both enjoy.

Calm and Quick

Usually injuries can be handled with common sense and a bandage.

When helping a child with an injury, stay calm but act quickly. If you panic or get excited, you will likely scare the child and make the problem worse. Think sensibly about the injury and decide the best way to fix it. You may need to call the child's parents or 911.

When dealing with illness, comfort the child and clean up any mess, like vomit. Call the child's parents. Although taking care of illnesses and injuries can be stressful, do your best to handle the situations.

CUTS AND SCRAPES

No matter what you do, kids may still fall and get injured. First aid for minor cuts and scrapes is pretty simple.

1. If you have plastic gloves, put them on or quickly wash your hands.
2. If the wound is bleeding, apply pressure with a moist paper towel until the bleeding stops.
3. Gently wash the wound with warm soapy water.
4. Put on an antiseptic cream, like Neosporin.
5. Cover with a bandage.
6. Wash your hands.

If the wound is deep, or won't stop bleeding after a few minutes, call 911 and the child's parents.

Handling Misbehavior

It would be great if children never misbehaved, but they do. The best way to handle misbehavior is to prevent it.

Set limits so kids know what they can and can't do, but be consistent. Children will be confused if you say no and later say yes. There are many different ways to handle a child who is misbehaving.

Being Positive

You can correct misbehavior by being positive. Try distracting the child with another acceptable activity choice. Instead of bringing up the child's bad behavior, praise him for a good behavior you've seen him do.

26

Ignoring

You can also try ignoring misbehavior. But you can't allow unsafe behavior. If a younger child has a tantrum and may hurt himself or someone else, stop him.

Warning System

Another option is calmly warning children what will happen if they continue misbehaving. If the behavior continues, be firm and enforce the rules.

Time-Outs

For older children, time-outs are very effective. After time-outs, welcome children back cheerfully. This shows that you still like them, but didn't like their behavior.

Helpful Hint

No matter how horribly a child is behaving, try to stay calm. If you can't control the situation, get help. Call the child's parents or your parents.

You've Got Skills!

You need certain skills for any job, especially babysitting. Now you know what skills you need to be a good babysitter. Use these skills to have a safe, fun time babysitting kids of all ages.

Checklist:

Qualities of a Super Sitter

Parents expect a lot from a babysitter. A babysitter takes care of someone very precious to parents—their child! Some of the best babysitters have these skills and traits:

✓ responsibility

✓ honesty

✓ patience

✓ dependability

✓ respect

✓ ability to remain calm and focused under pressure

✓ alertness

✓ friendliness

✓ creativity

✓ knowledge about children and their development

✓ completion of a babysitting course

✓ CPR certification

✓ ability to change diapers

✓ experience holding a baby

✓ can bottle feed and burp babies

✓ ability to deal with crying

✓ can handle misbehavior

Glossary

consistent (kuhn-SISS-tuhnt)—maintaining the same rules over time

CPR (cardiopulmonary resuscitation) (kar-dee-oh-PUHL-muh-nair-ee ree-se-se-TAY-shuhn)—a method of restarting a heart that has stopped beating; CPR involves breathing into a patient's mouth and pressing on a patient's chest in a certain rhythm.

enforce (en-FORSS)—to make sure something happens

Heimlich maneuver (HIME-lik muh-NOO-ver)—a safety procedure used to help someone who is choking

tantrum (TAN-truhm)—a fit of bad temper

toddler (TOD-lur)—a young child who is learning or has just learned to walk

Quick Tips

* A baby may spit-up while you're burping or bottle-feeding him. Use water and baking soda to remove a spit-up stain.

* Stay organized by keeping track of all your activities, including babysitting, on a personal calendar.

* If parents suggest time-outs for misbehavior, make sure they're age-appropriate. For each year of the child's age, add one minute to a timer.

Read More

Brown, Harriet. *The Babysitter's Handbook: The Care and Keeping of Kids.* Middleton, Wis.: Pleasant Company, 1999.

Fine, Jil. *Baby-sitting Smarts.* Smarts. New York: Children's Press, 2002.

Murkoff, Heidi Eisenberg. *The What to Expect Baby-sitter's Handbook.* New York: Workman, 2003.

Zakarin, Debra Mostow. *The Ultimate Baby sitter's Handbook: So You Wanna Make Tons of Money?* Los Angeles: Price Stem Sloan, 1997.

Internet Sites

FactHound offers a safe, fun way to find Internet sites related to this book. All of the sites on FactHound have been researched by our staff.

Here's how:

1. Visit *www.facthound.com*

2. Choose your grade level.

3. Type in this book ID **0736864660** for age-appropriate sites. You may also browse subjects by clicking on letters, or by clicking on pictures and words.

4. Click on the **Fetch It** button.

Facthound will fetch the best sites for you!

About the Author

Wendy Ann Mattox began babysitting at age 12. Her love for children continued to bloom as she grew up. As an adult, she is now married and the mother of four lovely daughters. She is a preschool teacher and freelance writer. She writes articles and books for children and about children.

Wendy believes that babysitting can help prepare anyone to become a better parent. And babysitting may even lead a person into an exciting career in teaching children or writing. It did for her!

Index